ANTI-DISTRACTION

ANTI-DISTRACTION

Bulletproof Mentality

For

ANTI-DISTRACTION

Quick Methods to Not Get Distracted

Instafo

instafo

ISBN 978-1-089-61190-5

Printed in the United States of America

First Edition

CONTENTS

Chapter 1: Detouring into Distraction

1.1 The Elusive Sin..9

1.2 Assignment: Recall from Back Burner........................12

Chapter 2: Creating a Mental Defense System for Distraction

2.1 Set Up Your Subconscious Firewall............................15

2.2 Color-Coded Anti-Distraction Security System.........16

2.3 Passive External and Active Internal..........................18

2.4 Assignment: Colors to the Rescue..............................20

Chapter 3: Preventing Distraction from Popping Up

3.1 Map Out an Anti-Distraction Plan of Attack............21

3.2 Assignment: Stick to a Plan.......................................24

Chapter 4: Diverting Distraction while in the Driver's Seat

4.1 Another Pathway to Explore......................................25

4.2 Anti-Distraction Emblems Embellishment................26

4.3 Distraction Intervention...............................29

4.4 Program a 3-Way Path Alert.......................31

4.5 Assignment: Rebounding from Roadblocks...............33

Chapter 5: Bypassing Distraction with Self-Motivation

5.1 Power of Words...35

5.2 Anti-Distraction Affirmative Action............................37

5.3 Assignment: Project Yourself Positively.....................40

Chapter 6: Blocking Out Distraction with Acoustical Science

6.1 The Anti-Distraction Effect of Binaural Sounds........41

6.2 Assignment: Optimize Brain for Concentration.........45

Chapter 7: Pulling Out All the Arsenals Against Distraction

7.1 Assignment 1: Pre-Planned Actions..........................47

7.2 Assignment 2: Color-Coded Implantation................48

7.3 Assignment 3: Visual Directions...........................49

7.4 Assignment 4: Assertive Affirmations......................50

7.5 Assignment 5: Brain Waves Alteration........................51

Chapter 8: Rerouting Away from Distraction

8.1 Drifted off Course...53

8.2 Back on Track..54

ANTI-DISTRACTION

Chapter 1:

Detouring into Distraction

The Elusive Sin

We've all been there. You have something important to finish on a deadline, and you're determined to get it done. *Then, suddenly, bam!* Something distracts you. Maybe you were working on your computer and decided to take a "quick" peek at Facebook, Twitter, or another cute cat video on YouTube. Then, you went down that rabbit hole of social media, and your project wound up on the back burner and an entire day went bye-bye.

This type of <u>distraction</u> does more than waste time. It likely makes you tired – or more tired than you already are. What gives? While working can leave you stressed, not working can leave you depressed.

So, what do you do in such predicament? Well, as obvious as it sounds, you'll have to get rid of this type of distraction as soon as possible. Putting off an important project to later in the day or beyond is a bad idea. There's no guarantee that you will be able to regain all your focus when you finally turn back to the project.

Also, keep in mind that distraction will lead you to the following consequences:

- **Distraction stops you from reaching your goals.** Some people might think that they'll always be able to find enough energy when they get back to their project after being distracted. *But ask yourself:* How long does it take to build up the energy you need to complete something? And how many times do you

find yourself low on energy and being distracted?
Let's face it, the distraction has to go!

- **Distraction promotes laziness and lack of ambition.**
A lack of concentration, especially when not dealt
with, promotes laziness. When you fall into this
type of rut, you may never "think" about having any
type of ambition in your life. It is as simple as that.
If you are constantly distracted, you can't take the
time to really focus on important matters that need
personal diligence. For example, if you want to lose
a certain amount of weight over the course of three
months, you will need to set up a good plan and
stick to it. If you get lazy and don't take the plan
seriously, you'll never achieve your goal.

- **Distraction turns you into a very unreliable person.**
With a lack of concentration and all the
catastrophic outcomes that come with it (plus the
confusion and frustration that may arise if you aren't
getting anything done), you will turn into someone

with a bad attitude and reputation, perhaps in both your professional and personal life.

Distractions are like certain infections or diseases that are totally debilitating you and preventing you from having your usual abilities and being fully functional. And like with most infections, you will need a good remedy as soon as possible in order to get your life back.

Assignment: Recall from Back Burner

Here's a small assignment for you:

1. Set an alarm for three hours later for the completion time of this little exercise.

2. Your assignment will consist of reciting the sentence, "The birds are flying in the rain today" <u>nine times</u> (<u>three times</u> *every hour*) until the alarm finally goes off. You can continue to go about your day as normal, but just try to remember the assignment when each hour

comes. For instance, you can say the sentence at the beginning of each hour, within 5-10 minutes of each hour, or towards the end of each hour; it doesn't matter as long as consistency is maintained.

3. Evaluate how well you were able to stay on course of what needed to be done? Did you remember to repeat the sentence <u>three times</u> within each hour? Did you actually repeat the sentence <u>nine times</u> total? Or did you completely forget about the assignment after a while because of your lack of concentration?

4. Make a note of the things that led you to lose your concentration. A text message? Social media? Music? Other people? Overall laziness?

The little experiment will not only show you how easy it is for you to get and stay distracted, but it will also shed some light on what it is that distracts you most of the time.

When you are done with this assignment you can move on to the next section.

Chapter 2:

Creating a Mental Defense System for Distraction

Set Up Your Subconscious Firewall

To start tackling this problem of distraction, we will start at the deep level of the subconscious mind to set up a natural defense system for your subconscious to automatically battle distraction.

But first, a quick question: How does your subconscious typically communicate to you?

<u>Hint</u>: Think of dreams because dreaming occurs from the subconscious.

<u>Answer</u>: It communicates to you through imagery and other abstract visuals; hence, the best way to communicate back to your subconscious is to also use imagery and abstract visuals, like two people speaking the same language.

Our first theory has to do with color because we believe that colors are easier to remember due to their strong visual impressionability. And for most of us, when we think of a color, we think of a particular object or image.

We'll apply this theory to colors for now, and later we'll explore how to do the same thing using images.

Color-Coded Anti-Distraction Security System

The idea behind this strategy is quite simple. First, you will have to pick <u>two colors</u>: **one** that will represent *"distractions* *or lacking focus"* and **another one** that will represent *"productivity or staying active."*

Follow these steps:

1. Pick your <u>two colors</u>. The **dull color** can represent your moments of distraction, which we will call your *"numbing moments."* Your **bright color** can represent your moments of full productivity, which we will call your *"pumping moments."*

For example, if you picked **gray** as the color representing your numbing moments, and **orange** as the color representing your pumping moments, you will then have to assimilate them as new mental concepts. Print out the <u>two colors</u> on pieces of paper so that they represent two color cards (that will be used for this). Make sure the cards are not too small; they can be squares of 8 x 3 inches each. They can simply be stored-bought colored flashcards.

2. While comfortably seated, start sliding your **first card** across the table. As the card passes in front of you from left to right, visualize in your head what it represents. So, if it's the **gray card**, the words *"numbing moment equals big distraction"* should come to your mind.

Do the same thing with the next card. As the **orange card** passes in front of your eyes, think of the words *"pumping moment equals being productive."*

3. Repeat the process <u>nine more times</u>, making sure you take your time to really facilitate the process.

Passive External and Active Internal

There are two approaches to this strategy depending on the urgency and on whichever is more convenient for you:

Passive External: Try it with your first task of the day. Regardless of what you are doing, place the **orange card** in front of you so that you can see it or have a glimpse of it, even when your eyes are directed somewhere else such as your computer or perhaps a pile of clothing you are folding. If you ever want to take a break, replace the **orange card** with the **gray card**, which allows you to be distracted and numbed to productivity.

Active Internal: You can also use the colors (without the cards) as a way to stimulate yourself as soon as you start feeling distracted. For example, if you are typing on your computer or mowing the lawn, as soon as you start doing something other than what you are supposed to do (like watching videos while you should be typing, or looking at your phone while you should be working on the lawn), think to yourself, *"I am on the* **gray** *and being distracted."* Then think **orange** (or whatever bright color you've selected), which will move you to a more productive attitude instantly because of what it represents or make you feel.

Assignment: Colors to the Rescue

Now the next part is for you to try applying mental colors at work.

- Use the more **active internal version** with the colors stored in your mind to immediately condition your concentration level;
- Or use the **passive external version** with the color-coded cards, where the dull card represents your lack of focus or concentration and the bright card represents your ability to be productive or active.

Chapter 3:

Preventing Distraction from Popping Up

Map Out an Anti-Distraction Plan of Attack

Sometimes, concentration has everything to do with planning and following through with a plan. Let's explain. Just like a ship's crew needs guidance by listening to and executing the orders of their captain, you also need to discipline yourself by applying a plan.

However, this may not be applicable to everybody, especially for those whose cause of distraction is from a diagnosed symptom like "**attention deficit hyperactivity** disorder (ADHD)." If that's the case, this may not apply to you - then follow the other strategies instead for staying focused in the current moment.

This planned-out conduct will be more like a path that you should take, and here are the steps you can follow to set up this path:

1. Make a list of the things that need to get done.

2. Next, draw two points on a piece of paper, one on the left side of the sheet, and the other on the right. One will be the starting point, and the other the endpoint. Next to the starting point, write *"Me Right Now."* Next to the endpoint, write the goal you need to accomplish.

3. Draw a line from the **starting point** to the **endpoint,** and along it write down all the steps that are needed to go from the starting point to the endpoint. For instance, if you had to sew a costume for Halloween, your

starting point would be "Me Right Now," and your endpoint would be "Costume Completed." Between the **two points**, draw a <u>line</u> that will count steps like:

Me Right Now => *set up the tool* => *sketch out the costume* => *get all the measurements ready* => *choose the right fabric* => *draw, measure, and cut pieces of the costume on the fabric* => *organize the pieces* => *decide which piece to sew first* => *sew the rest of the pieces* => *then sew the whole costume together* => **Costume Completed**

As you start working on your project, make sure you keep the paper with the path nearby and cross out the steps you are progressively completing. This method allows you to stay your course. It also allows you to work faster, which is better than when you just work without a grounded plan.

With this approach, it is like you are being the manager of yourself, setting up and delegating the tasks that need to be done, and then completing them.

Assignment: Stick to a Plan

Now train yourself and get accustomed to setting up a tangible path via written down. For some practice, simply imagine what are all the steps that you would do if you were actually assigned with the following:

- Decorating a wedding venue.

- Filling in an Excel spreadsheet with 2,000 names and addresses in alphabetical order.

Chapter 4:

Diverting Distraction while in the Driver's Seat

Another Pathway to Explore

Hey, you. Yes, you! Are you still paying attention? Don't worry. Everyone can get distracted. Even the brightest folks can lose their focus at some point. The lack of concentration has nothing to do with how bright you are. At its core, concentration has to do with *how truly determined you are.*

So, how do you stay determined if you have problems concentrating? Good question. And the key lies in choosing the right path.

Our next strategy consists of defining <u>three distinctive paths</u> that will clearly separate you from moderate to big distractions.

Remember when we talked about implanting color associations into our subconscious to ward of distraction? This time we will take it further using visual imagery. Here is how you will progress with this.

Anti-Distraction Emblems Embellishment

Familiarize yourself with <u>three distinct paths</u> that will keep you in a **complete focus state**, a **semi-distracted state**, and a **highly distracted state**, respectively.

You can use our examples below or create your own.

<u>Complete Focus State</u>: Think of the first path as a **straight line** or an **arrow**, which symbolizes going forward or staying focused on your current task.

<u>Semi-Distracted State</u>: The second path should symbolize you being partially distracted. Think of this path as a **bent line with an arrow**.

<u>Highly Distracted State</u>: The third and last path can be called the **spiraled path** and characterizes you being highly distracted.

Now, here is some more detail about each path:

- The first one - which is the straight path - represents you being 100% focused and demonstrates your ability to shut off completely from any type of distraction until your task is complete.

- The second one - the bent path - is characterized by a very brief moment of distraction, with an *"uh-oh"* moment, where you realize that you have wandered away from your initial task. The distraction is very short and can last from just a few minutes up to about 30 minutes.

- The last one - which is the spiraled path - represents a very long moment where you are exposed to any type of distraction for a very long time *(more than 30 minutes)*. Here, your *"uh-oh"* moment happens a bit too late when you actually remember about the task you are supposed to complete.

Distraction Intervention

We will use a few example scenarios to illustrate these three paths better.

Example one, the straight path: You are perfectly focused. The image of this path strictly guides you towards your goal, which should be to complete a given task. There is no *"uh-oh"* moment here.

Example two, the bent path: You've started working on your task but then you stop and start chatting with your friend about something. Then, 20 minutes later, you have an *"uh-oh"* moment, where you realize that you have neglected your work a little bit, so the bent path appears in your mind showing you that you are starting to take a wrong turn. So, you decide to get back to work, following the straight path once again.

Example three, the spiraled path: You have completely forgotten about the task and are now chilling, sitting on a chair with your legs crossed, sipping a glass of wine and laughing with your friends. Then, two hours later, you have an *"uh-oh"* moment where you remember that you did have something to do. That's when the image of the spiraled path invades your reality, signaling you that you have completely succumbed to distractions and that things are not looking too good for you as of the moment. Then, you decide to get back to work and follow a straight-working path again.

Program a 3-Way Path Alert

Now that we have given you examples to illustrate the different paths, let's see how you can memorize them and use them depending on the situation you are in.

1. Draw the **three paths** with their <u>names</u> underneath each of them.

2. Embed them into your mind one after the other. Start with the **straight path** *while covering* the **two others** with your hand. *Proceed the same way* with **second** and **third paths** by staring at each image for <u>60 seconds</u> (without blinking).

3. After <u>three minutes</u>, you can resume blinking. Next, repeat the process <u>five more times</u> covering the two other images while you are embedding each one.

Ensure that you cover the entire image, including the name.

4. Now "carry" these paths with you during the day while you complete your activities. You can also take a few minutes to condition yourself first thing in the morning or right before you start an activity. You can visualize the images a few times for 60 seconds each just to refresh your mind, even though you already know what they represent by now.

The ideas behind all these work like traffic signals with their *three colors* (red, yellow, green) that tell you when to move your car. You know that when the signal turns yellow, you need to slow down because it's about to turn red. When the light turns red, you stop. When it turns green, you go.

In comparison, the *green light* represents your **straight path**, which means go ahead and carry on! The *yellow light* represents the **bent path**, which means you have slowed down and that you risk being completely stopped. And lastly, the *red light* represents the **spiraled path**, where you have stopped being productive because you have totally surrendered to distractions.

Or even think of it like a GPS reminder where you have a destination in mind with whatever needs to get done, and the moment you venture off-course, the GPS kicks in alerting you that you're going the wrong way.

Assignment: Rebounding from Roadblocks

Now that you are starting to get the hang of these concepts, apply them today with your next activity.

Remember that thanks to these designs that you have already consciously embedded into your mind, you will have a subconscious *"uh-oh"* moment every time you wander away from your original path *(which is the straight path)*. Then, seeing the path that characterizes your level of distraction *(bent path or spiraled path)* will indicate the

<u>severity</u> of your sudden lack of focus. Have fun letting each one of these paths freeze you in your track as soon as you get your *"uh-oh"* moment and lead you to go back to path number one - the straight path.

Time to evaluate the effectiveness of this strategy by rating how focused and on track *(according to your activity)* you have become. Rate from a scale of <u>one</u> to <u>10</u> how you felt before applying your distraction alert reminder and after applying it.

Chapter 5:

Bypassing Distraction with Self-Motivation

Power of Words

Words may seem like nothing more than superficial sounds or lump of texts stringed together, but they truly have deeply profound, almost magical effects on our psyche. Think how chanting incantation, power of prayer, and support group discussion can elevate our moods and behaviors.

Transitively, most of the time we gain our motivation from positive words either verbally from others, visually from seeing them, or internally from our thoughts that can work miracles on our concentration level.

While distraction can stem from any myriad of causes, most of the time, it is due to fatigue or lack of immediate motivation.

With that said, what you are going to do here is use the power of <u>five motivational or affirmative assertions</u>. List five good things you have accomplished in your life. They don't all have to be huge accomplishments. Small ones are okay, but make sure they are all positive.

- They should be clear, in simple and short sentences, and a great motivational tool for you. For example, *"I have accomplished X in 10 minutes," "I was able to help Y to graduate last year,"* or *"I cooked dinner for 20 people last Christmas all by myself."*

- Read this list every time you *"wander away"* from a current task or goal for too long. As we said, fatigue and lack of motivation are detrimental, so reminding yourself of a few things you've accomplished will motivate you to break through your state of stagnancy.

- You should read the five accomplishments, one after the other, as a way to "illuminate" your brain all of the sudden, which should turn you from someone who is distracted to someone who is fired up wanting to accomplish even more because upon reminding you that you have done it before, you can repeat the process to replicate the success.

Anti-Distraction Affirmative Action

Let's go over an example to show how all this works.

Imagine that you are an English-to-Spanish translator. You've just received a 5,000-word document to translate in three days. You are aware that the work being assigned to you is enormous. But at the same time, you do not want to disappoint your employer. You start working on this file, but after only 100 words translated, you start "wandering away" and watching random short-clip videos one after the other on YouTube. The next thing you know, you've watched videos for two hours even though you know you need to complete the work in three days and are wasting time. What should you do to regain your concentration?

1. Start by creating five affirmative assertions, such as:

- "I have done this type of work before with more words and a similar deadline."
- "I have a great reputation because I work hard."
- "I always get great results."
- "I never gave up."
- "When I was a child, people used to say that I was a winner."

2. Use these phrases at the very beginning of the task, so they are almost like magic spells that will conjure

your laser focus. If you begin to lose your focus and concentration during the task, recite these positive statements.

To it sum up: When you are starting some necessary work, say the five magical phrases to get an instant boost of concentration. Then, whenever you are tempted in doing something else instead of working hard, say them once more to boost your concentration. Carry on this way until you knock it out of the park.

View this as someone trying to take the stairs to reach an office on the top floor of a tall building. The stairs represent the task at hand *(in this case, completing the translation in three days)*, and the office is the end result and everything positive that comes with it *(getting paid for your job, obtaining more recommendations from your employer, etc.)*.

Assignment: Project Yourself Positively

Your assignment now is simple but immensely effective for the long haul.

Create <u>five positive affirmative claims</u> about yourself. Use these affirmations to motivate yourself and help keep yourself engaged with what needs to be done until you cross that finish line.

Chapter 6:

Blocking Out Distraction with Acoustical Science

The Anti-Distraction Effect of Binaural Sounds

White noises are often used in modern-day healthcare applications to treat issues like anxiety, depression, hyperacusis or to help camouflage the annoyance caused by tinnitus (ringing in the ears).

The other interesting thing about white noises, or **binaural beats sounds,** is that they can help isolate you from background noises (especially in a public environment). This helps push your brain to focus more by completely "shutting off" from outside distractions, hence being very useful when it comes to blocking out distraction.

On a small historical note, binaural sounds were discovered in 1839 by Prussian physicist and meteorologist Heinrich Wilhelm Dove and have been widely used to help people sleep, improve their hearing, and help them be more productive with demanding projects.

Now, there are normally <u>five types</u> of binaural waves or sounds that affect brain waves. But, since we are dealing with concentration, we will focus on the ones that are supposed to keep you awake and focused like:

- **The alpha waves,** which range from <u>8</u> to <u>14hz</u>, can help you:

- Feel relaxed and focused.

- Reduce your stress.

- Promote positive thinking.

- Promote accelerated learning.

- Engage in action without a lot of effort.

Example of alpha waves:

www.youtube.com/watch?v=ZrGrYyScwjQ

- **The beta waves,** ranging from <u>14</u> to <u>30hz</u>, can help you:

- Have more focused attention.

- Develop a high level of cognition.

- Develop analytical thinking and the ability to be a problem solver.

- Be directed towards action.

Example of beta waves:

www.youtube.com/watch?v=mR3F4bAUU_s

- **The gamma waves,** ranging from <u>30</u> to <u>100hz</u>, can help you:

- Have a high level of information processing.

- Enhance your cognitive abilities.

- Have great memory recall.

- Sharpen your awareness.

- Be in transcendental states.

Example of gamma waves:

www.youtube.com/watch?v=EVPLIZotdrg

Assignment: Optimize Brain for Concentration

How do you use these <u>three types</u> of binaural waves anyway? It can be broken up into two phases:

- For phase one, you listen to the binaural beats while working and let the waves take over your mind and guide you through a successful day of productive work.

- For phase two, you listen to the waves while doing nothing for about an hour like a meditation session prior to jumping into your work.

Your chosen waves depend on the type of activity you have - the alpha waves are for smooth activities, beta waves for moderately smooth activities, and the gamma waves for rough or demanding activities.

Pick a random wave (alpha, beta, or gamma). Answer the following questions:

- After listening to your wave of choice, what is on your mind? Are you fixated towards a certain idea? Explain. (*This is to see if you are able to keep your focus even longer after listening to your wave of choice.)

- Does listening to the wave make you want to be active? What do you feel like doing while you are simply listening to them without any work in mind? Explain. (*This is to see if the waves can suddenly push you back into action with little or no effort.)

After this assignment, you should use the binaural waves during an activity but also as a warm-up tool (to put you in the right active frame of mind beforehand).

Now that we have armed you with all these helpful tools and strategies, let's put them into action.

Chapter 7:

Pulling Out All the Arsenals Against Distraction

Assignment 1: Pre-Planned Actions

Prevent and avoid distractions by having prior engagements to keep you occupied, like a to-do map or list.

1. Write down a list of activities that need to be done.

2. Use a piece of paper where you will draw a starting point and an endpoint across the piece of paper.

3. Draw a line between the starting point and the endpoint.

4. Write all the steps that are needed to go from the starting point to the endpoint.

5. As you start working through this path, make sure you keep the map handy and mark off the steps as you complete them.

Assignment 2: Color-Coded Implantation

Assimilate different colors into your subconscious to help you stay focused and effective for a long time by:

1. Picking your two colors (representing *numbing moments* vs. *pumping moments*). Get some flashcards or sticky notes that are not too small; they can be squares of 8 x 3 inches each.

2. While comfortably seated, start sliding your first card on the table in front of you. As it slides slowly on the table from left to right, visualize in your head what it represents. So, if it's the dull-colored card, the words *"numbing moment equals big distraction"* should also come to your mind.

3. Do the same thing with the next card, which is the bright-colored card, sliding it right in front of your eyes, with the words *"bright moment equals being productive"* also crossing your mind.

4. Repeat the process <u>nine more times</u> making sure you take your time to really facilitate and complete the process.

Assignment 3: Visual Directions

Eliminate distraction by drawing and following an activity path using images or other abstract visuals.

If you haven't memorized our example visual paths yet, line them up now in front of you and review them one at a time.

Remember, your initial path to follow should be the straight path. Then, let them redirect you to the original (desired) path by letting your *"uh-oh"* moment reveal the actual path that you have followed while being distracted (the bent path or the spiraled path), leading you back to a more focused state of mind with the straight path.

Assignment 4: Assertive Affirmations

Create <u>five affirmative claims</u> that will help you boost your confidence and motivation and keep you from losing concentration.

Keep these helpful tips in mind:

- The claims should be short and to the point.

- They don't have to be supernatural traits that only a superhuman could do.

- They should be accomplishments that made you feel proud of yourself.

- Say these five affirmations before you begin your activity and repeat them every time you start becoming distracted.

Assignment 5: Brain Waves Alteration

Read over the benefits of the <u>three different binaural waves</u> that we mentioned. Use either alpha, beta, or gamma waves to tune out distractions from now on and evaluate your progress by measuring how fast you complete a task *(in minutes or hours)* and how focused you are now *(from low level to high level)*.

This is how you should design your work or activity session with beta waves:

1. Warm up by listening to your choice of binaural wave (alpha, beta, or gamma depending on your need and on how focused you wish to be). Listen for <u>five minutes</u> while keeping your eyes closed.

2. After <u>five minutes</u> or so, begin your activity until it is completed.

Chapter 8:

Rerouting Away from Distraction

Drifted off Course

Everybody knows that distractions can affect how we perform in the short and long term, both during our childhood and also as adults. Children sometimes catch a break for criticism over their lack of attention span because they are still learning, and their parents are taking care of them.

But if you frequently succumb to distraction as an adult, the consequences can have a negative impact on your life. Your work and relationships will suffer because you don't know how to prioritize and manage those things that matter.

You will realize just how much time and energy are constantly being wasted that you'll never get back. In fact, you will eventually wake up one day and see your entire life has passed you by and you will regret never having lived to the fullest.

Back on Track

Luckily, there are simple ways to prevent distraction, maintain focus, and get things done with methods involving color-coded cards (or mental color implantation), which will definitely keep your mind from wondering more than anything else.

You can also use your self-accomplishment affirmations as a way to boost your concentration level. And, an activity path or binaural sounds can also help you shut off completely from distraction, helping you stay focused on the task and get more things done in record time.

Finally, you can kiss and kick your distraction goodbye with all that you have learned to get your concentration back, pay laser-focus attention, and experiment with of all these new and innovative strategies and become the most productive person you've always dreamed of being.

ANTI-DISTRACTION